Table Of Contents

Chapter 1: Navigating the Security Maze: A Comprehensive Guide to Mergers & Acquisitions 4

    Understanding the Security Landscape in Mergers & Acquisitions 5

    Key Players in M&A Security 7

    Common Security Risks in M&A Transactions 8

Chapter 2: Cybersecurity Considerations in M&A 11

    Cyber Due Diligence 12

    Data Breach Response Planning 14

    Cyber Insurance in M&A Transactions 14

Chapter 3: Compliance and Regulatory Challenges in M&A 17

    Regulatory Landscape in M&A Security 18

    Compliance Due Diligence 19

    Navigating International Regulations in M&A Transactions 21

Chapter 4: Data Privacy Considerations in M&A 24

    Protecting Sensitive Data in M&A Transactions 25

    GDPR Compliance in M&A Security 26

    Data Privacy Laws in Different Jurisdictions 28

Chapter 5: Due Diligence Best Practices in M&A Security 30

- Conducting a Comprehensive Security Due Diligence 31
- Identifying Red Flags in M&A Transactions 33
- Due Diligence Tools and Technologies 35
- Chapter 6: Integration of Security Systems Post-Merger 38
  - Merging Security Cultures 39
  - Integrating Security Technologies 40
  - Post-Merger Security Audit 41
- Chapter 7: Risk Management Strategies for M&A Security 45
  - Identifying and Assessing Risks 46
  - Mitigating Security Risks in M&A Transactions 47
  - Crisis Management in Security Breaches 49
- Chapter 8: Cultural Alignment and Security in M&A 52
  - Cultural Due Diligence in M&A Transactions 53
  - Building a Strong Security Culture Post-Merger 55
  - Addressing Cultural Differences in Security Practices 56
- Chapter 9: Vendor and Third-Party Risk Management in M&A 58
  - Vendor Due Diligence in M&A Transactions 59
  - Monitoring Third-Party Security Risks 61
  - Vendor Security Agreements in M&A Transactions 63
- Chapter 10: Employee Training and Awareness in M&A Security 65
  - Importance of Security Training for Employees 66

Creating a Security Awareness Program	67
Employee Responsibilities in M&A Security	68
Chapter 11: Legal Implications of Security Breaches in M&A	71
Legal Framework for Security Breaches in M&A	72
Liability in M&A Security Breaches	72
Legal Remedies for Security Breaches in M&A Transactions	73

01

Chapter 1: Navigating the Security Maze: A Comprehensive Guide to Mergers & Acquisitions

Understanding the Security Landscape in Mergers & Acquisitions

In the fast-paced world of mergers and acquisitions (M&A), it is crucial to have a comprehensive understanding of the security landscape. M&As involve a complex web of financial, legal, and operational considerations, and security risks must be carefully navigated to ensure a successful deal. This subchapter aims to provide insight into the various security challenges that can arise during M&As, and offer practical strategies for managing and mitigating these risks.

One of the key considerations in the security landscape of M&As is cybersecurity. As organizations become increasingly interconnected, the risk of cyber attacks and data breaches has become a top concern for businesses. In the context of M&As, cybersecurity considerations must be carefully evaluated to ensure that sensitive data is protected throughout the deal process. This includes conducting thorough due diligence on the cybersecurity practices of target companies, and implementing robust security measures to safeguard data during the integration process.

Compliance and regulatory challenges also play a significant role in the security landscape of M&As. In today's global business environment, companies must navigate a complex web of regulations and standards related to data privacy, intellectual property, and industry-specific requirements. Failure to comply with these regulations can result in costly fines and damage to reputation. As such, it is essential for organizations involved in M&As to conduct thorough compliance assessments and develop a comprehensive strategy for managing regulatory risks.

Data privacy considerations are another critical aspect of the security landscape in M&As. With the increasing amount of personal and sensitive data being exchanged during M&As, organizations must ensure that data privacy laws are upheld and that customer information is protected. This includes implementing robust data encryption measures, conducting privacy impact assessments, and establishing clear policies and procedures for data handling.

Due diligence best practices are also a key component of the security landscape in M&As. Due diligence is the process of assessing the financial, legal, and operational risks associated with a potential M&A transaction. In the context of security, due diligence involves evaluating the cybersecurity practices, compliance status, and data privacy measures of target companies. By conducting thorough due diligence, organizations can identify and mitigate potential security risks before they become major issues post-merger.

Securing the Deal: Navigating Mergers & Acquisitions Security

Overall, understanding the security landscape in M&As is essential for navigating the complex web of risks and challenges that can arise during the deal process. By focusing on cybersecurity, compliance, data privacy, due diligence, and other key security considerations, organizations can effectively manage security risks and ensure a successful M&A transaction. With careful planning and a proactive approach to security, organizations can protect their valuable assets and achieve their strategic objectives in the dynamic world of M&As.

Key Players in M&A Security

When it comes to mergers and acquisitions (M&A), there are key players involved in ensuring the security of the deal. These individuals play a crucial role in navigating the complex landscape of M&A security and mitigating risks that could potentially jeopardize the success of the transaction. Understanding the roles and responsibilities of these key players is essential for anyone looking to engage in M&A activities.

One of the most important key players in M&A security is the Chief Information Security Officer (CISO). The CISO is responsible for overseeing the organization's overall security posture and ensuring that all cybersecurity considerations are taken into account throughout the M&A process. They play a critical role in identifying potential risks and vulnerabilities, as well as developing strategies to address them effectively.

Another key player in M&A security is the legal team. Legal professionals are essential for navigating the compliance and regulatory challenges that often arise during M&A transactions. They ensure that all legal implications of security breaches are addressed and that the organization remains in compliance with relevant laws and regulations. The legal team also plays a crucial role in conducting due diligence and assessing the potential risks associated with the deal.

Data privacy considerations are another important aspect of M&A security, and the Chief Privacy Officer (CPO) plays a key role in this area. The CPO is responsible for ensuring that all data privacy laws and regulations are adhered to throughout the M&A process. They work closely with the legal team to assess the data privacy risks associated with the transaction and develop strategies to mitigate these risks effectively.

In addition to these key players, risk management professionals are also essential for M&A security. Risk managers are responsible for identifying, assessing, and mitigating risks that could impact the success of the deal. They work closely with the CISO, legal team, and CPO to develop comprehensive risk management strategies that address all potential threats to the organization's security.

Overall, understanding the roles and responsibilities of these key players is essential for navigating the security maze of M&A transactions successfully. By working together effectively, these individuals can help ensure that the organization remains secure throughout the M&A process and that the deal is completed successfully with minimal risk.

Common Security Risks in M&A Transactions

In the fast-paced world of mergers and acquisitions (M&A), security risks are a common concern for both buyers and sellers. Understanding these risks is crucial for ensuring a successful transaction and protecting sensitive information. In this subchapter, we will explore some of the most common security risks in M&A transactions and provide strategies for mitigating them.

One of the biggest security risks in M&A transactions is the potential for data breaches. During the due diligence process, sensitive information is shared between the parties involved, increasing the risk of unauthorized access. Cybersecurity considerations are essential in protecting this data and ensuring that it remains confidential throughout the transaction.

Compliance and regulatory challenges also pose a significant risk in M&A transactions. Different industries and countries have varying regulations regarding data privacy and security, making it essential for both parties to ensure they are in compliance with all relevant laws. Failure to do so can result in legal consequences and reputational damage.

Data privacy considerations are another critical aspect of M&A security. Ensuring that personal and sensitive information is handled appropriately and securely is essential for protecting the interests of both parties involved in the transaction. Implementing strong data privacy policies and procedures can help mitigate the risk of data breaches and ensure compliance with relevant regulations.

Securing the Deal: Navigating Mergers & Acquisitions Security

Due diligence best practices are essential for identifying and mitigating security risks in M&A transactions. Thoroughly assessing the security posture of the target company can help uncover any vulnerabilities and inform decision-making throughout the transaction process. Integration of security systems post-merger is also crucial for ensuring a seamless transition and protecting against potential security threats.

In conclusion, understanding and addressing security risks in M&A transactions is essential for ensuring a successful deal and protecting sensitive information. By considering factors such as cybersecurity, compliance, data privacy, due diligence, and post-merger integration, parties can mitigate risks and safeguard their interests throughout the transaction process. By prioritizing security and implementing best practices, companies can navigate the complexities of M&A transactions with confidence and resilience.

Securing the Deal: Navigating Mergers & Acquisitions Security

02

Chapter 2: Cybersecurity Considerations in M&A

Cyber Due Diligence

Cyber due diligence is a critical component of the overall due diligence process in mergers and acquisitions (M&A). In today's digital age, cyber threats are becoming increasingly prevalent, making it essential for organizations to assess and mitigate cybersecurity risks before finalizing a deal. Cyber due diligence involves evaluating the target company's cybersecurity posture, identifying potential vulnerabilities, and assessing the impact of any security breaches on the M&A transaction.

One of the key aspects of cyber due diligence is understanding the target company's existing cybersecurity infrastructure and practices. This includes assessing the effectiveness of their security controls, such as firewalls, intrusion detection systems, and encryption protocols. It is important to determine whether the target company has implemented industry best practices and compliance standards to protect their sensitive data from cyber threats.

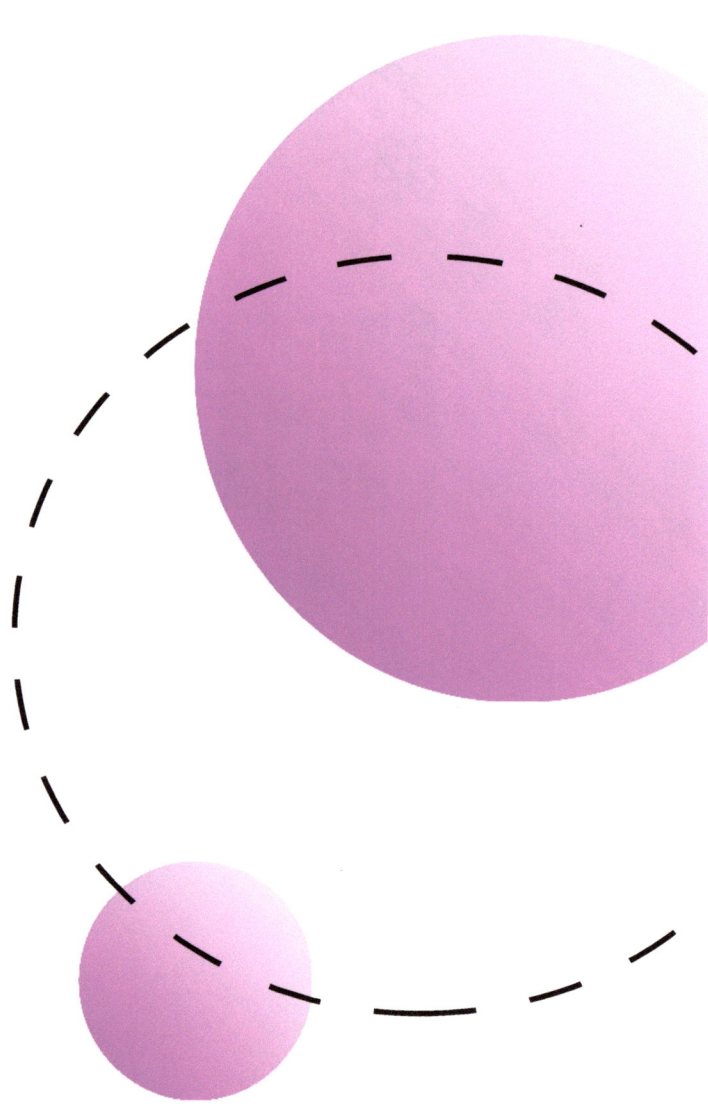

Securing the Deal: Navigating Mergers & Acquisitions Security

Another important consideration in cyber due diligence is identifying any past security incidents or breaches that the target company may have experienced. Understanding the nature and scope of these incidents can help assess the potential financial and reputational risks associated with the target company's cybersecurity posture. It is also crucial to evaluate how the target company responded to these incidents and whether they have implemented measures to prevent future breaches.

In addition to evaluating the target company's cybersecurity practices, cyber due diligence also involves assessing the potential impact of a security breach on the M&A transaction. This includes evaluating the financial and legal implications of a data breach, as well as the impact on the target company's reputation and customer trust. Understanding these risks can help the acquiring company make informed decisions about the deal and implement appropriate risk management strategies to protect their investment.

Overall, cyber due diligence is a critical step in the M&A process that cannot be overlooked. By conducting a thorough assessment of the target company's cybersecurity posture, identifying potential vulnerabilities, and evaluating the impact of security breaches, organizations can better protect themselves from cyber threats and ensure a successful and secure M&A transaction.

Securing the Deal: Navigating Mergers & Acquisitions Security

Data Breach Response Planning

Data Breach Response Planning is a crucial aspect of Mergers and Acquisitions security, as it helps organizations prepare for and respond effectively to potential data breaches. In today's digital age, data breaches are becoming increasingly common, and the consequences can be severe for organizations involved in M&A transactions. By having a well-thought-out data breach response plan in place, companies can minimize the impact of a breach and protect their valuable assets.

One of the first steps in Data Breach Response Planning is to establish a clear chain of command and designate specific roles and responsibilities for key individuals within the organization. This ensures that everyone knows their role in the event of a breach and can act quickly and decisively to contain the situation. It is also important to have a communication plan in place, both internally and externally, to ensure that all stakeholders are kept informed throughout the response process.

Another key component of Data Breach Response Planning is conducting regular training and drills to test the effectiveness of the plan and ensure that employees are prepared to respond appropriately in the event of a breach. This includes training on how to identify and report potential security incidents, as well as how to contain and mitigate the impact of a breach. By regularly testing the plan through simulated exercises, organizations can identify any weaknesses and make necessary adjustments to improve their response capabilities.

In addition to preparing for a potential breach, organizations should also have a robust incident response team in place to coordinate the response efforts. This team should include representatives from IT, legal, compliance, and communication departments, as well as external experts such as cybersecurity consultants and legal counsel. Having a dedicated incident response team ensures that the organization can respond quickly and effectively to contain the breach and minimize the impact on the business.

Overall, Data Breach Response Planning is a critical component of Mergers and Acquisitions security, as it helps organizations prepare for and respond effectively to potential data breaches. By establishing a clear chain of command, conducting regular training and drills, and having a dedicated incident response team in place, organizations can minimize the impact of a breach and protect their valuable assets. It is essential for organizations involved in M&A transactions to prioritize data breach response planning to safeguard their business and maintain trust with stakeholders.

Cyber Insurance in M&A Transactions

Cyber Insurance in M&A Transactions

Securing the Deal: Navigating Mergers & Acquisitions Security

Cybersecurity is a critical consideration in today's M&A transactions, as data breaches and cyber attacks can have a significant impact on the success of a deal. One way to mitigate the risks associated with cybersecurity threats is through cyber insurance. Cyber insurance can help protect both buyers and sellers in M&A transactions by providing coverage for financial losses resulting from data breaches, cyber attacks, and other cyber-related incidents.

For people trying to understand Mergers and Acquisitions and Security Risks, it is essential to recognize the importance of cyber insurance in M&A transactions. Cyber insurance policies can vary significantly in terms of coverage, limits, and exclusions, so it is crucial for both buyers and sellers to carefully review and negotiate the terms of their cyber insurance policies before completing a deal. By understanding the scope of coverage provided by their cyber insurance policies, buyers and sellers can better protect themselves from the financial consequences of cybersecurity threats.

Navigating the Security Maze: A Comprehensive Guide to Mergers & Acquisitions emphasizes the importance of incorporating cyber insurance into the overall security strategy for M&A transactions. Cyber insurance can help fill gaps in traditional insurance coverage by specifically addressing the unique risks associated with data breaches and cyber attacks. By including cyber insurance in their overall security strategy, buyers and sellers can better protect themselves from potential financial losses resulting from cybersecurity incidents.

Compliance and regulatory challenges in M&A transactions can be complex, especially when it comes to cybersecurity. Cyber insurance can help buyers and sellers navigate these challenges by providing coverage for fines and penalties resulting from non-compliance with data protection regulations. By including cyber insurance in their risk management strategy, buyers and sellers can better ensure compliance with data protection regulations and avoid costly regulatory penalties.

Securing the Deal: Navigating Mergers & Acquisitions Security

In conclusion, cyber insurance plays a critical role in M&A transactions by providing coverage for financial losses resulting from cybersecurity threats. By understanding the importance of cyber insurance and incorporating it into their overall security strategy, buyers and sellers can better protect themselves from the financial consequences of data breaches and cyber attacks. For people trying to understand Mergers and Acquisitions and Security Risks, it is essential to recognize the value of cyber insurance in mitigating the risks associated with cybersecurity threats in M&A transactions.

03

Chapter 3: Compliance and Regulatory Challenges in M&A

Securing the Deal: Navigating Mergers & Acquisitions Security

Regulatory Landscape in M&A Security

The regulatory landscape in M&A security is complex and constantly evolving, making it essential for businesses to stay informed and compliant with all relevant laws and regulations. Understanding the regulatory environment is crucial for successfully navigating the security risks involved in mergers and acquisitions. Regulatory requirements can vary significantly depending on the industry, jurisdiction, and the nature of the deal, so it is important to conduct thorough due diligence to ensure compliance.

One key consideration in the regulatory landscape of M&A security is the need to comply with data privacy regulations. With the increasing importance of data protection and privacy laws, businesses must carefully assess the data security practices of potential acquisition targets and ensure that they are in compliance with relevant regulations such as the General Data Protection Regulation (GDPR) or the California Consumer Privacy Act (CCPA). Failure to comply with data privacy regulations can result in significant financial penalties and reputational damage.

Securing the Deal: Navigating Mergers & Acquisitions Security

Another important aspect of the regulatory landscape in M&A security is understanding the legal implications of security breaches. Security breaches can have far-reaching consequences, including legal action, financial losses, and damage to reputation. Businesses must have robust security measures in place to prevent breaches, as well as a clear understanding of their legal obligations in the event of a breach. This includes notifying regulators, customers, and other stakeholders as required by law.

In addition to data privacy and security breach regulations, businesses engaging in M&A must also consider compliance and regulatory challenges in other areas such as anti-trust laws, intellectual property rights, and industry-specific regulations. Failure to comply with these regulations can result in regulatory scrutiny, fines, and even the rejection of the deal. Therefore, it is essential for businesses to conduct thorough due diligence and seek legal advice to ensure compliance with all relevant regulations.

Overall, navigating the regulatory landscape in M&A security requires a comprehensive understanding of the relevant laws and regulations, as well as proactive risk management strategies. By staying informed and compliant with all regulatory requirements, businesses can mitigate security risks and increase the likelihood of a successful merger or acquisition. It is crucial for individuals involved in M&A transactions to seek out expert advice and resources to help them understand and navigate the regulatory landscape effectively.

Compliance Due Diligence

Compliance due diligence is a critical aspect of the merger and acquisition process, ensuring that all parties involved are abiding by relevant laws, regulations, and industry standards. This step involves thoroughly assessing the legal and regulatory compliance of the target company to identify any potential risks or liabilities that could impact the deal. By conducting comprehensive compliance due diligence, acquirers can mitigate legal and financial risks, protect their reputation, and ensure a smooth integration process post-merger.

Securing the Deal: Navigating Mergers & Acquisitions Security

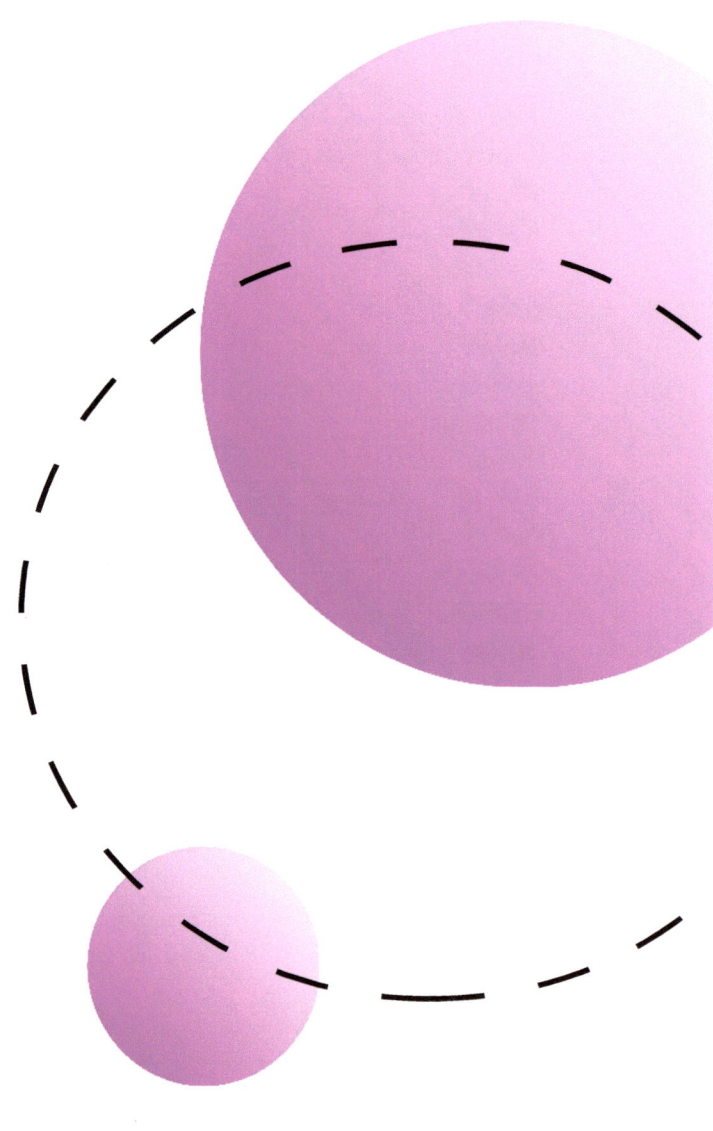

One of the key considerations in compliance due diligence is understanding the regulatory landscape in which the target company operates. This includes identifying any industry-specific regulations, as well as general legal requirements that may apply. By conducting a thorough review of the target company's compliance with these regulations, acquirers can assess the level of risk associated with the deal and make informed decisions about how to proceed.

In addition to regulatory compliance, it is important to consider other areas of compliance due diligence, such as data privacy and security. With the increasing threat of cyber attacks and data breaches, acquirers must ensure that the target company has robust data protection measures in place to safeguard sensitive information. Failure to address data privacy concerns during the due diligence process can result in significant regulatory fines and reputational damage post-merger.

Furthermore, compliance due diligence should also include an assessment of the target company's internal policies and procedures related to ethics and corporate governance. This includes reviewing employee training programs, whistleblower policies, and codes of conduct to ensure that the target company has a strong culture of compliance. By identifying any gaps or weaknesses in these areas, acquirers can take steps to address them during the integration process and minimize the risk of future compliance issues.

Securing the Deal: Navigating Mergers & Acquisitions Security

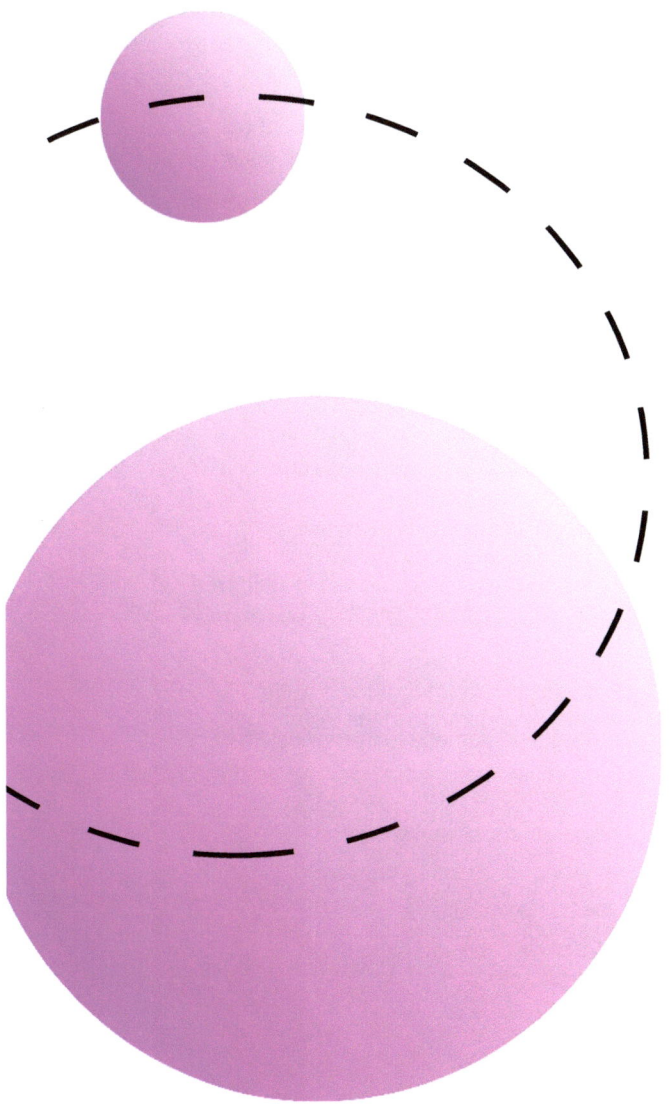

Overall, compliance due diligence is a critical component of the mergers and acquisitions process, helping acquirers to identify and mitigate potential risks related to legal and regulatory compliance. By conducting thorough due diligence in this area, acquirers can protect themselves from costly legal disputes, regulatory fines, and reputational damage, ensuring a successful and secure merger or acquisition transaction.

Navigating International Regulations in M&A Transactions

Navigating international regulations in M&A transactions can be a complex and daunting task, especially for those new to the world of mergers and acquisitions. Understanding the various regulations and compliance requirements in different countries is crucial to ensuring a successful deal. In this subchapter, we will explore the key considerations and challenges that arise when navigating international regulations in M&A transactions.

Securing the Deal: Navigating Mergers & Acquisitions Security

One of the most important aspects of navigating international regulations in M&A transactions is understanding the regulatory landscape in each country involved in the deal. This includes understanding the different laws and regulations that govern M&A transactions, as well as any potential changes or updates to these regulations. It is essential to work closely with legal experts who are well-versed in international M&A regulations to ensure compliance and mitigate any potential risks.

Another key consideration when navigating international regulations in M&A transactions is data privacy considerations. With the increasing focus on data privacy and protection, it is essential to understand the data privacy laws in each country involved in the deal. Failure to comply with these laws can result in significant fines and penalties, as well as damage to the reputation of the companies involved. Conducting thorough due diligence on data privacy practices is crucial to identifying any potential risks and addressing them proactively.

Compliance and regulatory challenges are also common when navigating international regulations in M&A transactions. Companies must ensure that they are in compliance with all relevant laws and regulations, including anti-corruption laws, competition laws, and export control regulations. Failure to comply with these laws can result in legal action, fines, and damage to the reputation of the companies involved. It is essential to conduct thorough due diligence to identify any potential compliance issues and address them before completing the deal.

Integration of security systems post-merger is another important consideration when navigating international regulations in M&A transactions. Companies must ensure that their security systems are integrated seamlessly to prevent any gaps or vulnerabilities that could be exploited by cybercriminals. This includes conducting thorough risk assessments, implementing robust security measures, and providing adequate training and awareness to employees. Failure to properly integrate security systems post-merger can result in data breaches, financial losses, and damage to the reputation of the companies involved.

In conclusion, navigating international regulations in M&A transactions requires a thorough understanding of the regulatory landscape, data privacy considerations, compliance and regulatory challenges, and integration of security systems post-merger. By working closely with legal experts, conducting thorough due diligence, and implementing robust security measures, companies can successfully navigate the complex world of international M&A transactions and mitigate any potential risks.

Securing the Deal: Navigating Mergers & Acquisitions Security

04

Chapter 4: Data Privacy Considerations in M&A

Protecting Sensitive Data in M&A Transactions

Protecting sensitive data in M&A transactions is a critical aspect of ensuring the success and security of the deal. With the increasing number of cyber threats and data breaches, it is essential for companies involved in M&A transactions to take proactive steps to safeguard their sensitive information. This subchapter will explore some key strategies and best practices for protecting sensitive data during M&A transactions.

One of the first steps in protecting sensitive data in M&A transactions is to conduct a thorough risk assessment. This involves identifying all potential risks and vulnerabilities that could compromise the security of the data. By understanding the potential threats, companies can develop a comprehensive security plan that addresses these risks and mitigates them effectively.

Another important aspect of protecting sensitive data in M&A transactions is to ensure that all parties involved in the deal are aware of the security protocols and procedures in place. This includes employees, vendors, and third parties who may have access to sensitive information. By providing training and raising awareness about the importance of security, companies can minimize the risk of data breaches and unauthorized access.

In addition to training and awareness, companies should also implement strong encryption and access controls to protect sensitive data during M&A transactions. This includes encrypting data at rest and in transit, as well as restricting access to sensitive information based on role and need-to-know basis. By implementing these security measures, companies can effectively protect their data from unauthorized access and cyber threats.

Furthermore, companies involved in M&A transactions should also consider the legal implications of security breaches. In the event of a data breach, companies may be subject to regulatory fines and lawsuits, which can have a significant impact on the deal. By understanding the legal implications of security breaches and taking proactive steps to prevent them, companies can minimize the risk of legal consequences and protect their reputation in the market.

Securing the Deal: Navigating Mergers & Acquisitions Security

Overall, protecting sensitive data in M&A transactions is a complex and multifaceted process that requires careful planning and execution. By following the strategies and best practices outlined in this subchapter, companies can effectively safeguard their sensitive information and ensure the success and security of the deal.

GDPR Compliance in M&A Security

In today's digital age, data privacy and security have become paramount concerns in the realm of mergers and acquisitions (M&A). With the implementation of the General Data Protection Regulation (GDPR) in 2018, companies engaging in M&A activities must now navigate a complex regulatory landscape to ensure compliance and mitigate risks. This subchapter will delve into the various aspects of GDPR compliance in M&A security, providing valuable insights for individuals seeking to understand the intersection of data privacy and M&A transactions.

Securing the Deal: Navigating Mergers & Acquisitions Security

One of the key challenges in achieving GDPR compliance in M&A security lies in the sheer volume of data that is exchanged during the due diligence process. As companies share sensitive information with potential acquirers, they must ensure that data protection measures are in place to safeguard against unauthorized access or disclosure. Failure to comply with GDPR regulations can result in hefty fines and damage to the reputation of the companies involved, making it imperative for M&A professionals to prioritize data privacy considerations throughout the transaction.

Moreover, the integration of security systems post-merger presents another hurdle for companies seeking GDPR compliance in M&A security. As two entities come together, they must align their data protection policies and procedures to ensure consistency and adherence to GDPR requirements. This process can be complex and time-consuming, requiring careful planning and coordination between legal, IT, and compliance teams to minimize potential vulnerabilities and ensure a smooth transition.

In addition to technical challenges, cultural alignment and security in M&A transactions also play a crucial role in GDPR compliance. Companies must assess the security posture and data privacy practices of their target companies to identify any potential gaps or risks that may impact the overall security of the combined entity. By conducting thorough due diligence and implementing robust risk management strategies, companies can mitigate security threats and protect sensitive data from breaches or unauthorized access.

Overall, GDPR compliance in M&A security requires a comprehensive and proactive approach to data privacy and security. By understanding the regulatory requirements, conducting thorough due diligence, and implementing appropriate security measures, companies can navigate the complexities of M&A transactions while safeguarding sensitive information and minimizing risks. With the right tools and strategies in place, M&A professionals can ensure GDPR compliance and enhance the security posture of their organizations in an increasingly interconnected and data-driven business environment.

Data Privacy Laws in Different Jurisdictions

Data privacy laws are an integral part of any merger and acquisition transaction, as they can have significant implications on the deal. Understanding the data privacy laws in different jurisdictions is crucial for companies looking to navigate the complex landscape of M&A security. In this subchapter, we will explore the various data privacy laws in different jurisdictions and their impact on M&A transactions.

One of the key considerations in M&A security is compliance with data privacy laws. Different jurisdictions have different regulations governing the collection, storage, and transfer of personal data. For example, the European Union's General Data Protection Regulation (GDPR) imposes strict requirements on companies handling personal data of EU residents. Failure to comply with these regulations can result in hefty fines and reputational damage.

In the United States, data privacy laws vary by state, with California leading the way with the California Consumer Privacy Act (CCPA). The CCPA gives consumers the right to know what personal data is being collected about them and the right to opt-out of the sale of their data. Companies involved in M&A transactions must ensure compliance with these laws to avoid legal and financial repercussions.

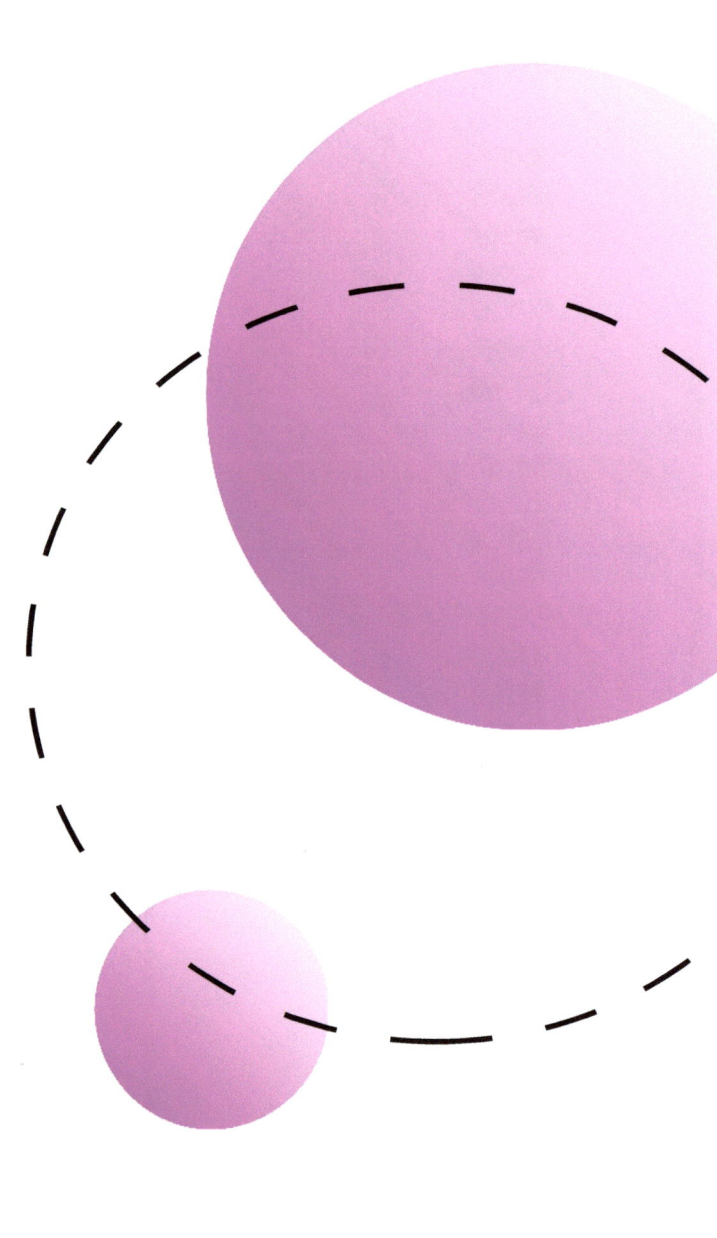

Securing the Deal: Navigating Mergers & Acquisitions Security

In Asia, data privacy laws are also evolving rapidly. Countries like Japan, South Korea, and Singapore have implemented data protection laws to regulate the handling of personal data. Companies engaging in M&A transactions in these jurisdictions must be aware of these laws to mitigate risks and ensure compliance. Overall, navigating the data privacy laws in different jurisdictions is a critical aspect of M&A security. Companies must conduct thorough due diligence to assess the data privacy risks associated with a potential merger or acquisition. By understanding and complying with these laws, companies can safeguard sensitive information, protect their reputation, and mitigate legal risks in the ever-changing landscape of M&A security.

05

Chapter 5: Due Diligence Best Practices in M&A Security

Securing the Deal: Navigating Mergers & Acquisitions Security

Conducting a Comprehensive Security Due Diligence

Conducting a comprehensive security due diligence is a crucial step in the process of mergers and acquisitions, especially in today's digital age where cybersecurity threats are rampant. This subchapter will delve into the importance of conducting thorough due diligence when it comes to security risks, and how it can help mitigate potential vulnerabilities and protect valuable assets.

One of the key aspects of conducting a comprehensive security due diligence is identifying all potential security risks and vulnerabilities within the target company. This includes assessing the company's cybersecurity infrastructure, compliance with regulations, data privacy practices, and overall risk management strategies. By conducting a thorough assessment, acquirers can better understand the potential security threats they may face post-merger and develop strategies to address them proactively.

In addition to identifying security risks, it is also important to assess the cultural alignment between the two companies when it comes to security practices. This includes evaluating the current security culture within the target company, as well as the willingness of employees to adhere to new security protocols post-merger. By ensuring that there is alignment in security culture, acquirers can minimize the risk of insider threats and other security breaches that may arise due to human error.

Another important aspect of conducting a comprehensive security due diligence is assessing vendor and third-party risk management practices within the target company. This includes evaluating the security protocols of third-party vendors who have access to sensitive company data, as well as assessing the potential risks associated with outsourcing certain security functions. By understanding the risks associated with third-party vendors, acquirers can better protect their assets and prevent potential security breaches.

Furthermore, it is essential to consider the legal implications of security breaches in mergers and acquisitions. This includes assessing the potential liabilities that may arise in the event of a security breach, as well as ensuring that all necessary legal protections are in place to mitigate these risks. By understanding the legal implications of security breaches, acquirers can better protect themselves from potential lawsuits and financial losses.

Securing the Deal: Navigating Mergers & Acquisitions Security

Overall, conducting a comprehensive security due diligence is essential for mitigating security risks in mergers and acquisitions. By assessing potential vulnerabilities, aligning security cultures, evaluating vendor risks, and understanding legal implications, acquirers can better protect their assets and ensure a smooth transition post-merger. It is crucial for people trying to understand mergers and acquisitions and security risks to prioritize security due diligence in order to navigate the complexities of the M&A process successfully.

Identifying Red Flags in M&A Transactions

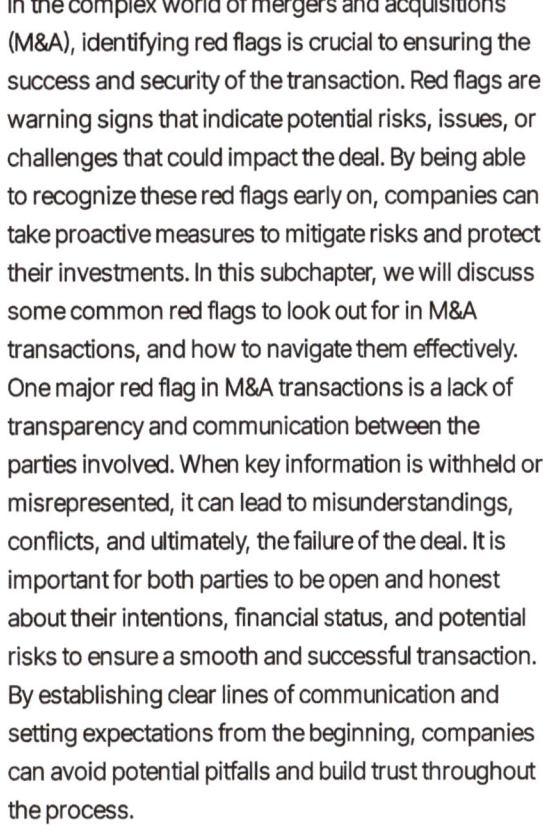

In the complex world of mergers and acquisitions (M&A), identifying red flags is crucial to ensuring the success and security of the transaction. Red flags are warning signs that indicate potential risks, issues, or challenges that could impact the deal. By being able to recognize these red flags early on, companies can take proactive measures to mitigate risks and protect their investments. In this subchapter, we will discuss some common red flags to look out for in M&A transactions, and how to navigate them effectively.

One major red flag in M&A transactions is a lack of transparency and communication between the parties involved. When key information is withheld or misrepresented, it can lead to misunderstandings, conflicts, and ultimately, the failure of the deal. It is important for both parties to be open and honest about their intentions, financial status, and potential risks to ensure a smooth and successful transaction. By establishing clear lines of communication and setting expectations from the beginning, companies can avoid potential pitfalls and build trust throughout the process.

Another red flag to watch out for in M&A transactions is regulatory compliance issues. Failure to comply with laws and regulations can result in costly fines, legal disputes, and damage to the company's reputation. It is essential for companies to conduct thorough due diligence and assess the regulatory landscape before proceeding with a transaction. By identifying compliance risks early on and implementing strategies to address them, companies can minimize potential legal liabilities and ensure a seamless transition post-merger.

Securing the Deal: Navigating Mergers & Acquisitions Security

Cybersecurity concerns are also a significant red flag in M&A transactions, especially in today's digital age where data breaches and cyber attacks are on the rise. Companies must assess the cybersecurity posture of their target companies and evaluate the risks associated with integrating their systems and networks. By prioritizing cybersecurity considerations in the due diligence process and implementing robust security measures post-merger, companies can protect their sensitive information and safeguard against potential threats.

Data privacy considerations are another important red flag to consider in M&A transactions, particularly with the increasing focus on data protection regulations such as the General Data Protection Regulation (GDPR). Companies must understand the data privacy implications of the transaction, including how personal data is collected, stored, and shared, and ensure compliance with relevant laws and regulations. By addressing data privacy concerns upfront and implementing appropriate safeguards, companies can mitigate risks and protect the privacy rights of their customers and stakeholders.

Securing the Deal: Navigating Mergers & Acquisitions Security

In conclusion, identifying red flags in M&A transactions is a critical step in navigating the complex security landscape of mergers and acquisitions. By being vigilant and proactive in assessing risks, communicating effectively, and addressing compliance, cybersecurity, and data privacy concerns, companies can secure the deal and achieve a successful outcome. By following best practices and seeking expert guidance where needed, companies can navigate the security maze of M&A transactions with confidence and ensure the protection of their investments and assets.

Due Diligence Tools and Technologies

Due diligence is a critical aspect of any merger or acquisition, as it involves a thorough investigation and analysis of the target company's operations, financials, and potential risks. In today's fast-paced and technology-driven world, due diligence tools and technologies play a crucial role in helping companies navigate the complex landscape of M&A security. These tools can range from advanced data analytics platforms to cybersecurity risk assessment software, all designed to provide valuable insights and mitigate potential risks.

One of the key due diligence tools in M&A security is cybersecurity risk assessment software, which helps companies identify and assess potential vulnerabilities in the target company's IT systems and infrastructure. By conducting a comprehensive cybersecurity risk assessment, companies can uncover any weaknesses in the target company's cybersecurity defenses and develop a plan to address them before completing the merger or acquisition. This can help prevent costly data breaches and security incidents down the line.

Another important due diligence tool in M&A security is compliance and regulatory monitoring software, which helps companies ensure that the target company is in compliance with all relevant laws and regulations. This includes data privacy laws, industry-specific regulations, and international standards for cybersecurity. By using compliance and regulatory monitoring software, companies can identify any potential compliance issues early on in the due diligence process and take steps to address them before they become a problem.

Securing the Deal: Navigating Mergers & Acquisitions Security

Data privacy considerations are also a key aspect of due diligence in M&A security. Companies must ensure that the target company has implemented robust data privacy practices and policies to protect sensitive information from unauthorized access or disclosure. Data privacy considerations in M&A due diligence involve assessing the target company's data protection measures, identifying any potential risks to data privacy, and developing a plan to mitigate those risks post-merger.

In conclusion, due diligence tools and technologies are essential for companies navigating the complex landscape of M&A security. By leveraging advanced data analytics platforms, cybersecurity risk assessment software, compliance and regulatory monitoring tools, and data privacy considerations, companies can identify potential risks early on in the due diligence process and take proactive steps to address them. This can help ensure a successful merger or acquisition and protect both companies from costly security breaches and compliance issues in the future.

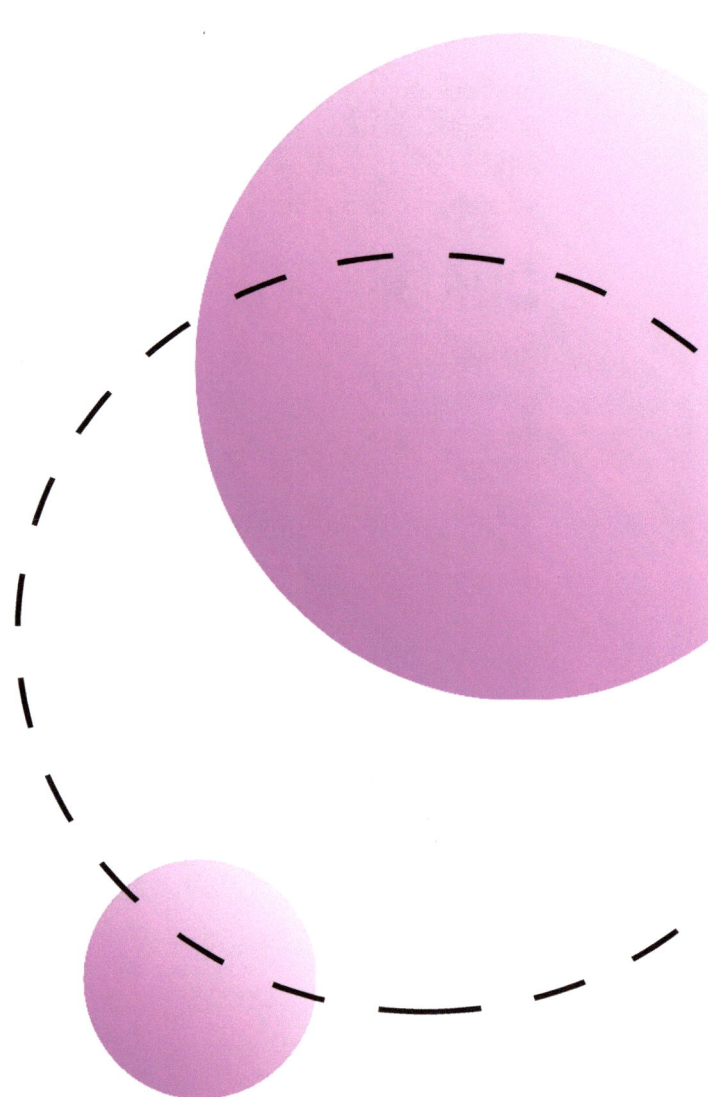

Securing the Deal: Navigating Mergers & Acquisitions Security

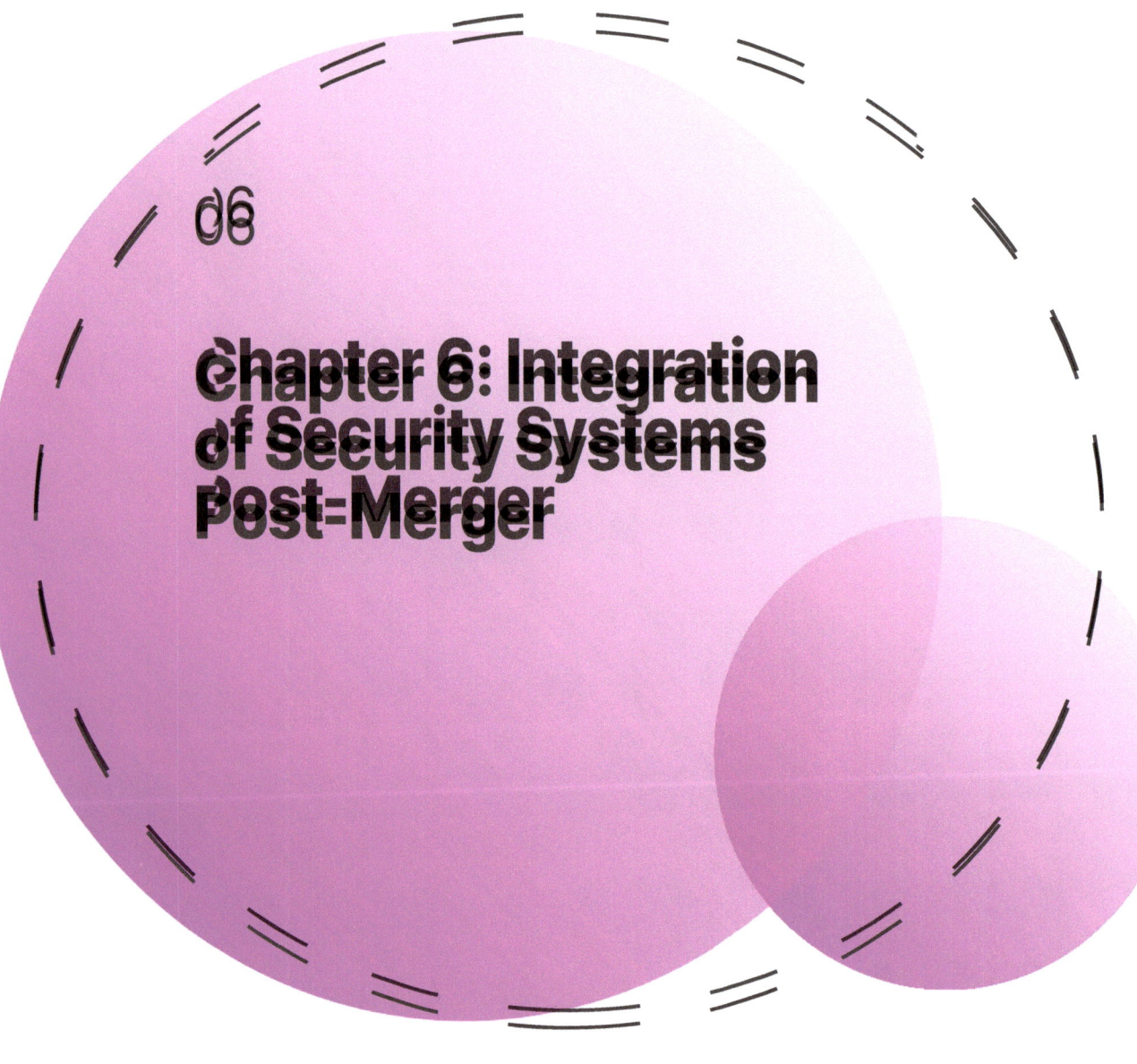

Chapter 6: Integration of Security Systems Post-Merger

Securing the Deal: Navigating Mergers & Acquisitions Security

Merging Security Cultures

When two companies come together through a merger or acquisition, one of the biggest challenges they face is aligning their security cultures. Each organization likely has its own unique approach to security, stemming from its history, industry norms, and leadership. Merging these distinct cultures can be a complex and delicate process, but it is essential for ensuring the security of the newly combined entity.

Navigating the Security Maze: A Comprehensive Guide to Mergers & Acquisitions

In order to successfully merge security cultures, it is crucial for both organizations to have a clear understanding of their respective security policies, procedures, and practices. This includes conducting a comprehensive assessment of each company's security posture, identifying any gaps or vulnerabilities, and developing a plan for integrating the two cultures. By taking a systematic approach to this process, organizations can minimize the risk of security breaches and ensure a smooth transition.

Cybersecurity considerations in M&A

One of the most pressing concerns when merging security cultures is cybersecurity. With the increasing sophistication of cyber threats, it is essential for organizations to have robust cybersecurity measures in place to protect their sensitive data and systems. This includes implementing strong encryption protocols, monitoring for suspicious activity, and training employees on best practices for cybersecurity. By prioritizing cybersecurity in the merger process, organizations can mitigate the risk of data breaches and other cyber attacks.

Compliance and regulatory challenges in M&A

Another key consideration when merging security cultures is compliance with industry regulations and legal requirements. Each organization may be subject to different regulatory frameworks, which can create challenges when trying to align security practices. It is important for organizations to conduct a thorough review of their compliance obligations, identify any potential conflicts, and develop a plan for addressing them. By staying ahead of compliance issues, organizations can avoid costly fines and legal disputes.

Data privacy considerations in M&A

Securing the Deal: Navigating Mergers & Acquisitions Security

Finally, organizations must also consider data privacy when merging security cultures. With the increasing focus on data protection and privacy rights, it is essential for organizations to have strong data privacy policies in place. This includes ensuring that sensitive data is encrypted, limiting access to confidential information, and providing employees with training on data privacy best practices. By prioritizing data privacy in the merger process, organizations can build trust with customers and stakeholders and avoid reputational damage.

Integrating Security Technologies

In today's fast-paced business environment, the integration of security technologies is crucial in ensuring a smooth transition during mergers and acquisitions. With the ever-evolving landscape of cybersecurity threats, it is essential for organizations to stay ahead of the curve by implementing advanced security measures to protect their data and assets. By integrating security technologies, companies can enhance their overall security posture and mitigate risks associated with M&A activities.

Securing the Deal: Navigating Mergers & Acquisitions Security

One of the key aspects of integrating security technologies is to ensure that the systems and processes of both organizations are compatible and can work seamlessly together. This requires a thorough assessment of the existing security infrastructure of both companies to identify any gaps or vulnerabilities that need to be addressed. By conducting a comprehensive audit, organizations can identify potential risks and develop a plan to integrate security technologies effectively.

Another important consideration when integrating security technologies is to establish clear communication channels between the IT and security teams of both organizations. This collaboration is essential in ensuring that all security protocols and measures are aligned to protect the newly merged entity from potential threats. By fostering a culture of collaboration and information sharing, organizations can strengthen their overall security posture and minimize the risk of security breaches.

Moreover, integrating security technologies post-merger requires a strategic approach that takes into account the unique needs and priorities of the newly merged entity. This may involve consolidating security systems, implementing new technologies, or updating existing protocols to align with the organization's security objectives. By taking a proactive approach to integrating security technologies, organizations can effectively manage security risks and protect their valuable assets.

In conclusion, integrating security technologies is a critical component of navigating the complex landscape of mergers and acquisitions. By implementing advanced security measures, organizations can safeguard their data, assets, and reputation from potential threats and vulnerabilities. By following best practices and fostering collaboration between IT and security teams, organizations can enhance their overall security posture and ensure a successful integration process post-merger.

Post-Merger Security Audit

Securing the Deal: Navigating Mergers & Acquisitions Security

One of the critical steps in the merger and acquisition process is conducting a post-merger security audit. This audit is essential for identifying any security vulnerabilities that may have arisen during the transition period. It helps ensure that the newly merged entity is secure and protected from potential threats. The post-merger security audit involves a thorough examination of the combined organization's security infrastructure, policies, and practices.

During the post-merger security audit, it is crucial to assess the effectiveness of the security systems and controls in place. This includes evaluating the organization's network security, data protection measures, access controls, and incident response procedures. By conducting a comprehensive audit, organizations can identify any gaps or weaknesses in their security posture and take corrective actions to mitigate risks.

Cybersecurity considerations play a significant role in the post-merger security audit. With the increasing number of cyber threats targeting organizations, it is essential to ensure that the merged entity's cybersecurity defenses are robust and up to date. This includes assessing the organization's vulnerability to cyber attacks, reviewing its security policies and procedures, and implementing necessary security measures to protect sensitive data and information.

Securing the Deal: Navigating Mergers & Acquisitions Security

Compliance and regulatory challenges are also a critical aspect of the post-merger security audit. Organizations must ensure that they are in compliance with relevant laws and regulations governing data privacy, security, and information protection. This includes assessing the organization's adherence to industry standards and best practices, as well as ensuring that any compliance gaps are addressed promptly.

In conclusion, the post-merger security audit is a crucial step in ensuring the security and protection of the newly merged entity. By conducting a thorough examination of the organization's security infrastructure, policies, and practices, organizations can identify and address any security vulnerabilities that may have arisen during the merger and acquisition process. This helps mitigate risks, protect sensitive data, and ensure compliance with relevant laws and regulations:

Securing the Deal: Navigating Mergers & Acquisitions Security

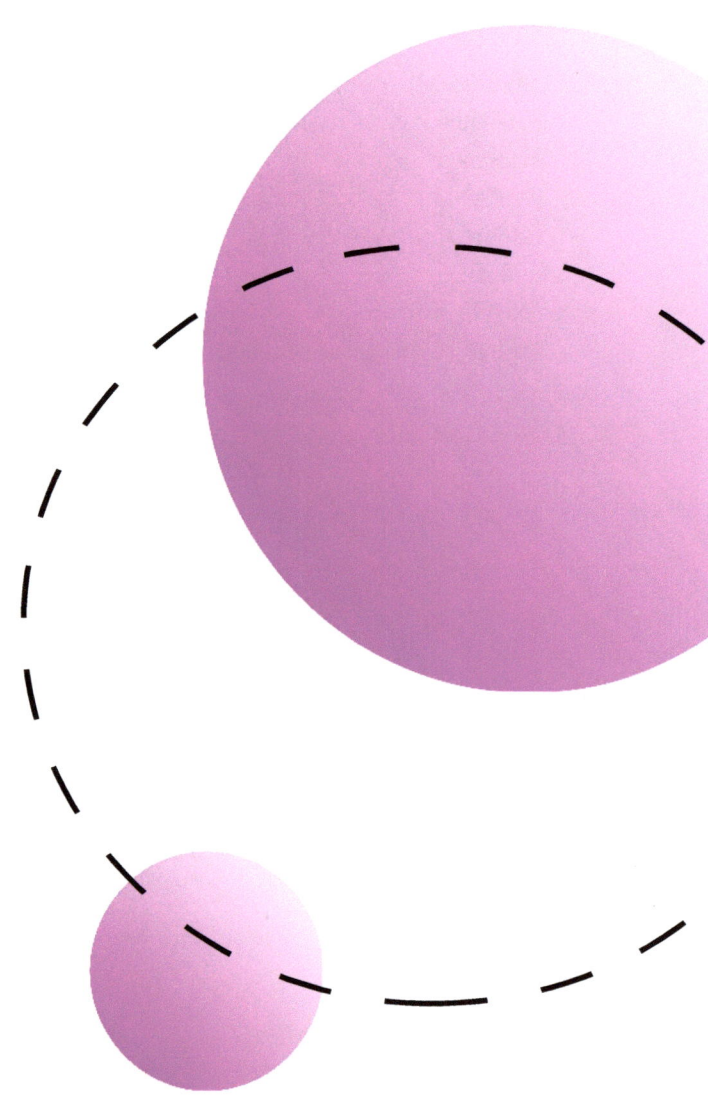

07

Chapter 7: Risk Management Strategies for M&A Security

Securing the Deal: Navigating Mergers & Acquisitions Security

Identifying and Assessing Risks

In the world of mergers and acquisitions (M&A), one of the most critical aspects that must be addressed is the identification and assessment of potential risks. Understanding the risks associated with a merger or acquisition is essential for ensuring the success of the deal and protecting the interests of all parties involved. Risks can come in many forms, including cybersecurity threats, compliance and regulatory challenges, data privacy concerns, and more. It is crucial for those involved in M&A transactions to have a comprehensive understanding of these risks and how to manage them effectively.

Navigating the Security Maze: A Comprehensive Guide to Mergers & Acquisitions

Navigating the complex security maze of mergers and acquisitions can be a daunting task. However, with the right knowledge and tools, it is possible to successfully navigate these challenges. From conducting thorough due diligence to integrating security systems post-merger, there are a variety of strategies that can be employed to mitigate risks and ensure the security of the transaction. By following a comprehensive guide to M&A security, individuals can better protect their interests and achieve a successful outcome.

Cybersecurity Considerations in M&A

Securing the Deal: Navigating Mergers & Acquisitions Security

Cybersecurity threats pose a significant risk to M&A transactions. As technology continues to advance, so do the tactics used by cyber criminals to exploit vulnerabilities and gain access to sensitive information. It is essential for those involved in M&A deals to prioritize cybersecurity considerations and implement robust security measures to protect against potential threats. By conducting thorough risk assessments and implementing best practices for cybersecurity, organizations can minimize the risk of data breaches and other security incidents that could compromise the success of the deal.

Compliance and Regulatory Challenges in M&A

Compliance and regulatory challenges are another key concern for those involved in M&A transactions. Failure to comply with relevant laws and regulations can result in significant legal and financial consequences for both parties. It is crucial for organizations to conduct thorough due diligence to identify any potential compliance issues and develop a strategy for addressing them. By working closely with legal and compliance experts, organizations can ensure that all regulatory requirements are met and minimize the risk of facing penalties or other repercussions.

Data Privacy Considerations in M&A

Data privacy is a growing concern in the digital age, with individuals and organizations alike increasingly focused on protecting their sensitive information. In the context of M&A transactions, data privacy considerations are particularly important, as the sharing of confidential information between parties can create vulnerabilities that could be exploited by malicious actors. By implementing strong data privacy policies and procedures, organizations can safeguard their data and ensure compliance with relevant privacy laws. Additionally, by prioritizing data privacy considerations throughout the M&A process, organizations can build trust with stakeholders and mitigate the risk of data breaches or other security incidents.

Mitigating Security Risks in M&A Transactions

Mitigating Security Risks in M&A Transactions

In the fast-paced world of mergers and acquisitions (M&A), security risks are a key concern for both buyers and sellers. These risks can range from cyber threats to compliance and regulatory challenges, making it essential for all parties involved to proactively address security concerns throughout the deal-making process. By implementing effective risk mitigation strategies, organizations can protect their assets and ensure a smooth transition post-merger.

Securing the Deal: Navigating Mergers & Acquisitions Security

One of the first steps in mitigating security risks in M&A transactions is conducting thorough due diligence. This involves assessing the security posture of the target company, identifying potential vulnerabilities, and evaluating the effectiveness of existing security controls. By taking a comprehensive approach to due diligence, organizations can uncover hidden risks and make informed decisions about whether to proceed with the transaction. Once a deal is finalized, it is crucial to integrate security systems seamlessly to minimize disruption to business operations. This involves aligning policies, procedures, and technologies to create a unified security framework that protects sensitive data and systems. By prioritizing security integration post-merger, organizations can prevent gaps in protection and ensure a secure transition for all stakeholders. Risk management strategies are also essential for mitigating security risks in M&A transactions. This involves identifying potential threats, assessing their likelihood and impact, and implementing controls to reduce risk exposure. By taking a proactive approach to risk management, organizations can protect their investments and safeguard against potential security breaches.

Cultural alignment is another key consideration in mitigating security risks in M&A transactions. This involves aligning the security practices and values of both organizations to create a cohesive security culture post-merger. By fostering a shared commitment to security, organizations can enhance collaboration, communication, and compliance, ultimately reducing the risk of security incidents.

In conclusion, mitigating security risks in M&A transactions requires a proactive and comprehensive approach. By conducting thorough due diligence, integrating security systems effectively, implementing risk management strategies, and fostering cultural alignment, organizations can protect their assets and ensure a secure transition post-merger. By prioritizing security throughout the deal-making process, organizations can navigate the complexities of M&A transactions with confidence and resilience.

Crisis Management in Security Breaches

Security breaches can have disastrous consequences for companies involved in mergers and acquisitions. It is essential for organizations to have a solid crisis management plan in place to effectively respond to and mitigate the impact of a security breach. This subchapter will explore the key components of crisis management in security breaches and provide guidance for organizations navigating the complexities of M&A security risks. One of the first steps in crisis management is to establish a dedicated incident response team. This team should be comprised of individuals with expertise in cybersecurity, legal, communications, and other relevant areas. Having a designated team in place ensures a swift and coordinated response to security breaches, minimizing the damage to the organization's reputation and bottom line. Communication is another critical aspect of crisis management in security breaches. Organizations must be transparent with stakeholders, including employees, customers, investors, and regulators, about the breach and its impact. Clear and timely communication can help restore trust and credibility in the organization's ability to handle security incidents effectively.

Securing the Deal: Navigating Mergers & Acquisitions Security

In addition to communication, organizations must also conduct a thorough investigation into the security breach to identify the root cause and prevent future incidents. This may involve working with external cybersecurity experts to assess the extent of the breach, remediate vulnerabilities, and implement security controls to strengthen the organization's defenses against future attacks.

Legal implications of security breaches in M&A are another important consideration in crisis management. Organizations must comply with data protection laws and regulations, such as GDPR and HIPAA, and notify affected individuals and authorities about the breach within specified timeframes. Failure to comply with legal requirements can result in significant fines and penalties, further exacerbating the impact of the security breach on the organization.

In conclusion, crisis management in security breaches is a critical component of M&A security risk management. By establishing an incident response team, communicating effectively with stakeholders, conducting a thorough investigation, and complying with legal requirements, organizations can effectively navigate the complexities of security breaches in mergers and acquisitions. By following best practices in crisis management, organizations can minimize the impact of security breaches and protect their reputation and bottom line in the aftermath of a cyber attack.

Securing the Deal: Navigating Mergers & Acquisitions Security

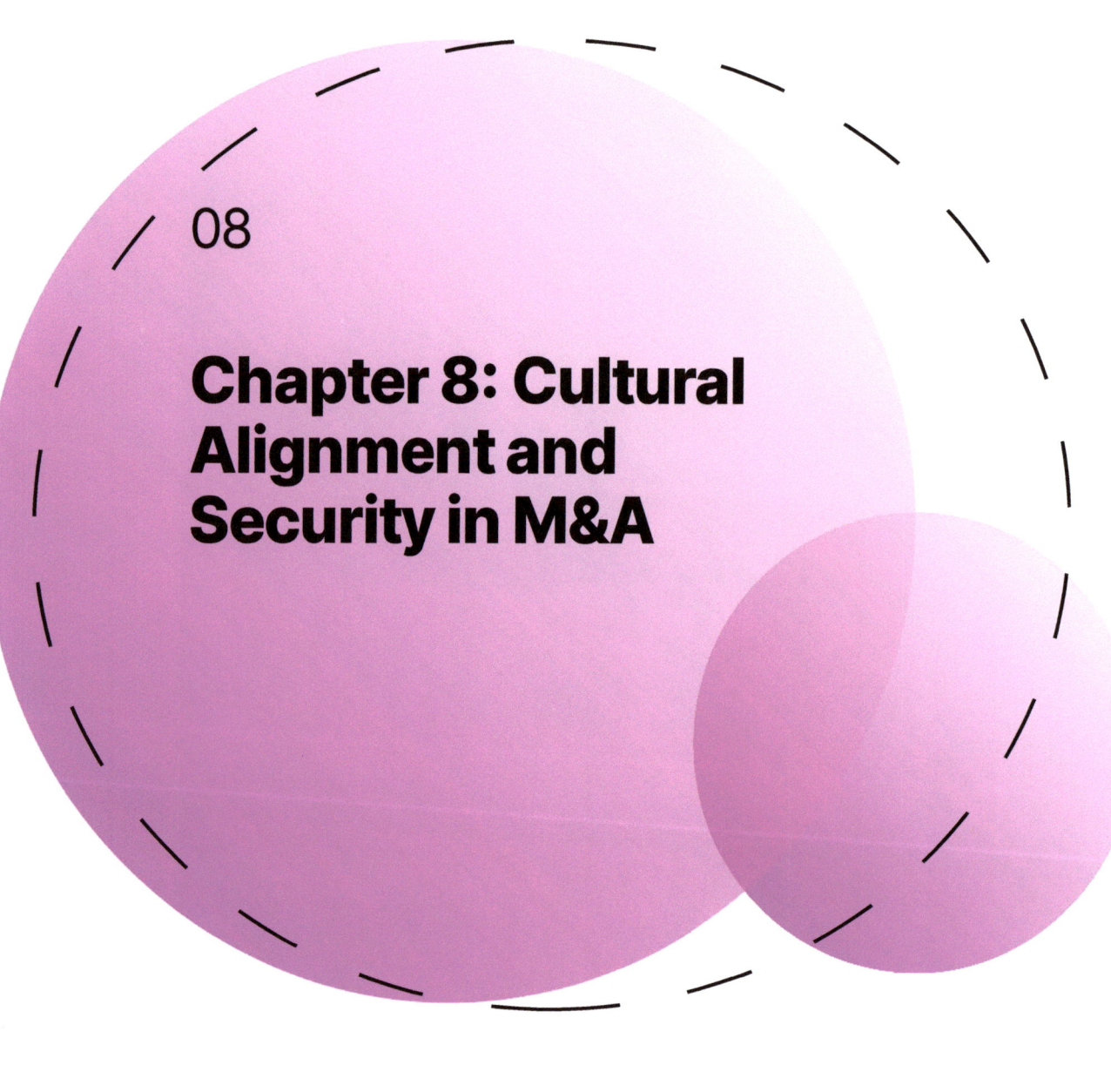
Chapter 8: Cultural Alignment and Security in M&A

Securing the Deal: Navigating Mergers & Acquisitions Security

Cultural Due Diligence in M&A Transactions

Cultural due diligence in M&A transactions is a crucial aspect that is often overlooked by many organizations. In today's globalized business environment, companies are increasingly engaging in cross-border M&A deals, which can bring about a clash of cultures and values. It is essential for companies to conduct thorough cultural due diligence to ensure a smooth integration process post-merger. This involves understanding the cultural nuances of the target company, identifying potential cultural conflicts, and developing strategies to mitigate these risks.

One of the key reasons why cultural due diligence is important in M&A transactions is because cultural misalignment can lead to employee disengagement, decreased productivity, and ultimately, the failure of the deal. By conducting cultural due diligence, companies can identify cultural differences early on and develop a plan to address them during the integration process. This can help to ensure a successful merger and create a cohesive organizational culture that aligns with the company's strategic goals.

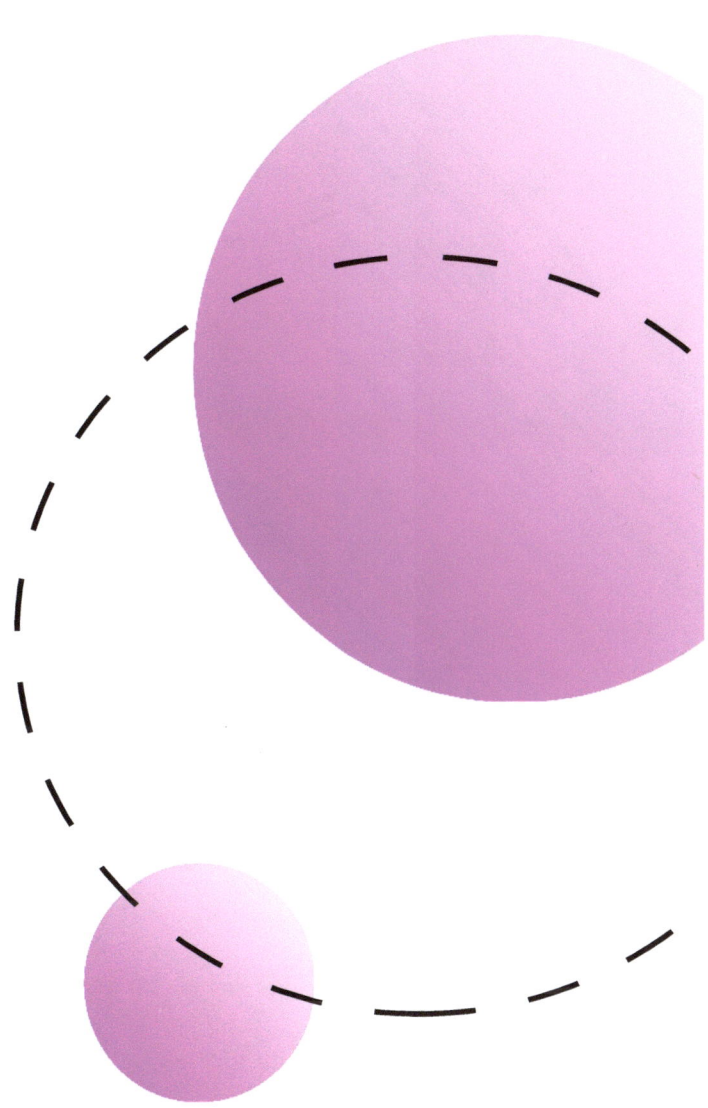

Securing the Deal: Navigating Mergers & Acquisitions Security

In addition to employee engagement and productivity, cultural due diligence also plays a significant role in managing security risks in M&A transactions. Cultural differences can impact the way employees perceive and respond to security policies and practices. By understanding the cultural norms and values of the target company, organizations can develop security strategies that are tailored to the specific needs of the combined entity. This can help to prevent security breaches and ensure the protection of sensitive data during the integration process.

Furthermore, cultural alignment and security in M&A transactions can also have legal implications. In today's regulatory environment, companies are held accountable for security breaches and data privacy violations. Failure to address cultural differences and security risks during the M&A process can result in hefty fines, legal disputes, and reputational damage. By conducting cultural due diligence and integrating security systems post-merger, organizations can mitigate these risks and ensure compliance with legal requirements.

Securing the Deal: Navigating Mergers & Acquisitions Security

In conclusion, cultural due diligence is a critical component of M&A transactions that should not be overlooked. By understanding the cultural nuances of the target company, identifying potential conflicts, and developing strategies to address them, organizations can ensure a smooth integration process, mitigate security risks, and comply with legal requirements. Cultural alignment and security in M&A transactions are essential for creating a cohesive organizational culture, maintaining employee engagement, and protecting sensitive data. By incorporating cultural due diligence into their M&A strategy, companies can secure the deal and navigate the complexities of mergers and acquisitions with confidence.

Building a Strong Security Culture Post-Merger

One of the most critical aspects of a successful merger or acquisition is ensuring that the security culture of both organizations is aligned and strengthened post-transaction. This is particularly important in today's increasingly digital world, where cyber threats are constantly evolving and becoming more sophisticated. In order to navigate the security maze that often accompanies M&A activity, it is essential for organizations to prioritize building a strong security culture that is focused on protecting sensitive data and safeguarding against potential breaches.

Cybersecurity considerations in M&A are paramount, as the merging of two organizations can create vulnerabilities that were not present before. It is crucial for companies to conduct thorough due diligence and assess the cybersecurity posture of both entities involved in the transaction. By identifying potential risks and vulnerabilities early on, organizations can develop a comprehensive security strategy that addresses any gaps and mitigates potential threats.

Compliance and regulatory challenges in M&A can also pose significant obstacles for organizations looking to merge or acquire another company. It is essential for companies to understand the regulatory landscape in which they operate and ensure that all security practices are in compliance with industry standards and regulations. By prioritizing compliance and regulatory adherence, organizations can avoid costly penalties and reputational damage that can result from non-compliance.

Data privacy considerations in M&A are another critical aspect of building a strong security culture post-merger. With the increasing amount of data being collected and stored by organizations, it is essential for companies to prioritize data privacy and protection. By implementing robust data privacy policies and procedures, organizations can ensure that sensitive information is safeguarded and that customer trust is maintained.

In conclusion, building a strong security culture post-merger is essential for navigating the complex world of M&A security. By prioritizing cybersecurity considerations, compliance and regulatory adherence, data privacy protection, and employee training and awareness, organizations can mitigate potential risks and vulnerabilities that may arise during the integration process. By aligning security practices and fostering a culture of security consciousness, organizations can ensure a smooth and successful transition post-merger.

Addressing Cultural Differences in Security Practices

When it comes to mergers and acquisitions, one of the key challenges that companies often face is addressing cultural differences in security practices. Different organizations may have varying approaches to security, which can create friction during the integration process. It is crucial for companies to recognize and understand these cultural differences in order to effectively navigate the security landscape post-merger.

One important aspect to consider when addressing cultural differences in security practices is communication. Companies must ensure that there is clear and open communication between all parties involved in the merger or acquisition. This includes discussing security policies, procedures, and best practices to ensure that everyone is on the same page. Failure to communicate effectively can lead to misunderstandings and potential security vulnerabilities.

Another important consideration is the alignment of security cultures. Companies must work to identify common ground and areas of overlap in their security practices. This may require compromise and flexibility on both sides to create a unified approach to security that meets the needs of the newly merged organization. By fostering a culture of collaboration and cooperation, companies can better integrate their security practices post-merger.

Securing the Deal: Navigating Mergers & Acquisitions Security

It is also essential for companies to conduct thorough due diligence on the security practices of the organizations involved in the merger or acquisition. This includes assessing the strengths and weaknesses of each company's security program, as well as identifying any potential gaps or vulnerabilities. By conducting a comprehensive security assessment, companies can better understand the cultural differences in security practices and develop a plan to address them effectively.

Ultimately, addressing cultural differences in security practices requires a proactive and strategic approach. Companies must be willing to invest time and resources into understanding the security cultures of the organizations involved in the merger or acquisition. By fostering open communication, aligning security cultures, conducting due diligence, and taking a proactive approach to security, companies can successfully navigate the complexities of merging security practices post-merger.

Chapter 9: Vendor and Third-Party Risk Management in M&A

Securing the Deal: Navigating Mergers & Acquisitions Security

Vendor Due Diligence in M&A Transactions

Vendor due diligence is a crucial aspect of M&A transactions that cannot be overlooked. When acquiring a company, the acquiring company must conduct a thorough investigation into the vendor's operations, financials, and security practices to ensure that there are no hidden risks or liabilities that could jeopardize the deal. This process involves assessing the vendor's compliance with regulations, cybersecurity measures, data privacy practices, and overall risk management strategies. By conducting due diligence on vendors, companies can mitigate potential security risks and ensure a smooth transition post-merger.

Securing the Deal: Navigating Mergers & Acquisitions Security

One of the key considerations in vendor due diligence is assessing the vendor's cybersecurity practices. With the increasing prevalence of cyber threats and data breaches, it is essential for companies to understand the security measures in place at their vendors to protect sensitive information. This includes evaluating the vendor's network security, data encryption protocols, incident response plans, and overall cybersecurity posture. By conducting a comprehensive assessment of the vendor's cybersecurity practices, companies can identify any vulnerabilities and address them before they become a major security concern post-merger.

In addition to cybersecurity considerations, companies must also assess the vendor's compliance with regulations and industry standards. This includes evaluating the vendor's adherence to data privacy laws, financial regulations, and other legal requirements that may impact the deal. By ensuring that the vendor is compliant with relevant regulations, companies can avoid potential legal liabilities and reputational damage in the event of a security breach or compliance violation. This due diligence process also helps companies identify any gaps in compliance and work with the vendor to address them before finalizing the deal.

Furthermore, vendor due diligence should also include an evaluation of the vendor's risk management strategies. This involves assessing the vendor's approach to identifying, assessing, and mitigating risks across their operations. By understanding the vendor's risk management practices, companies can determine whether the vendor is capable of managing potential security risks and implementing effective risk mitigation strategies. This allows companies to assess the overall risk profile of the vendor and make informed decisions about the level of risk associated with the deal.

Overall, vendor due diligence is a critical component of M&A transactions that can have a significant impact on the success of the deal. By conducting a thorough assessment of vendors' cybersecurity practices, compliance with regulations, and risk management strategies, companies can identify and mitigate potential security risks before they become a problem. This process not only helps protect sensitive information and assets but also ensures a smooth integration post-merger. By prioritizing vendor due diligence in M&A transactions, companies can navigate the complex security landscape and secure their deals effectively.

Monitoring Third-Party Security Risks

Monitoring third-party security risks is a crucial aspect of ensuring the overall security of a merger or acquisition deal. Third-party vendors and partners often have access to sensitive information and systems, making them potential weak points in the security posture of the combined entity. Therefore, it is essential for organizations involved in M&A activity to have a robust strategy in place for monitoring and managing third-party security risks.

One key consideration when monitoring third-party security risks is conducting thorough due diligence on potential vendors and partners. This includes assessing their security practices, policies, and controls to ensure they meet the same standards as the acquiring organization. Additionally, organizations should consider conducting regular security assessments and audits of third-party vendors to ensure ongoing compliance with security requirements.

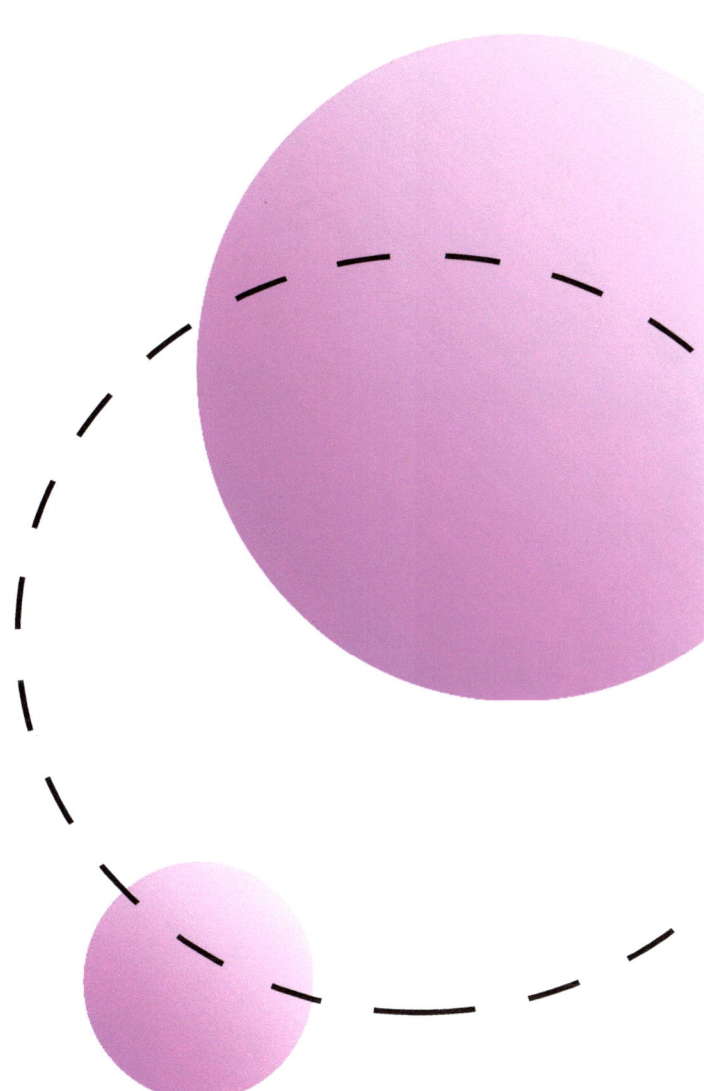

Securing the Deal: Navigating Mergers & Acquisitions Security

Another important aspect of monitoring third-party security risks is establishing clear contractual agreements that outline security responsibilities and expectations. These agreements should include provisions for data protection, breach notification, and incident response to ensure that both parties are aligned on security protocols and procedures. Regular monitoring of vendor compliance with these agreements is essential to mitigating security risks.

In addition to contractual agreements, organizations should also consider implementing technology solutions to monitor and assess third-party security risks. This may include using third-party risk management platforms or security information and event management (SIEM) systems to track and monitor vendor activities and potential security threats. By leveraging technology tools, organizations can gain real-time visibility into third-party security risks and proactively address any vulnerabilities.

Securing the Deal: Navigating Mergers & Acquisitions Security

Overall, monitoring third-party security risks requires a multi-faceted approach that includes due diligence, contractual agreements, and technology solutions. By taking a proactive stance on third-party security, organizations can better protect their sensitive information and systems during the M&A process. By implementing a comprehensive strategy for monitoring third-party security risks, organizations can enhance their overall security posture and minimize the potential for security breaches or incidents.

Vendor Security Agreements in M&A Transactions

When it comes to M&A transactions, vendor security agreements play a crucial role in mitigating risks and ensuring the security of both parties involved. These agreements outline the responsibilities and obligations of vendors in terms of cybersecurity, data protection, and compliance. By establishing clear guidelines for vendors, companies can better protect themselves against potential security breaches and regulatory challenges.

In M&A transactions, vendor security agreements should address a variety of key areas, including data privacy considerations, compliance with industry regulations, and risk management strategies. By including specific language regarding these issues in the agreement, companies can ensure that vendors are held accountable for maintaining the security of sensitive information and mitigating potential risks. Additionally, vendor security agreements should outline the procedures for monitoring and auditing vendor compliance to ensure ongoing security measures are in place.

One of the biggest challenges in M&A transactions is integrating security systems post-merger. Vendor security agreements can help facilitate this process by outlining the steps that vendors must take to align their security practices with those of the acquiring company. By establishing clear guidelines for integration, companies can minimize the risk of security gaps and ensure a smooth transition following the merger or acquisition.

Effective vendor and third-party risk management is essential in M&A transactions to safeguard against potential security breaches and mitigate risks. By including provisions in vendor security agreements that address risk management strategies, companies can better protect themselves against external threats and ensure the security of sensitive data. Additionally, vendor security agreements should include provisions for employee training and awareness to help prevent security incidents and ensure compliance with security protocols:

Securing the Deal: Navigating Mergers & Acquisitions Security

Overall, vendor security agreements are a critical component of M&A transactions, helping companies navigate the complex landscape of cybersecurity, compliance, and risk management. By establishing clear guidelines for vendors and third parties, companies can better protect themselves against security breaches, regulatory challenges, and data privacy concerns. By prioritizing security in vendor agreements, companies can mitigate risks and ensure a successful outcome in M&A transactions.

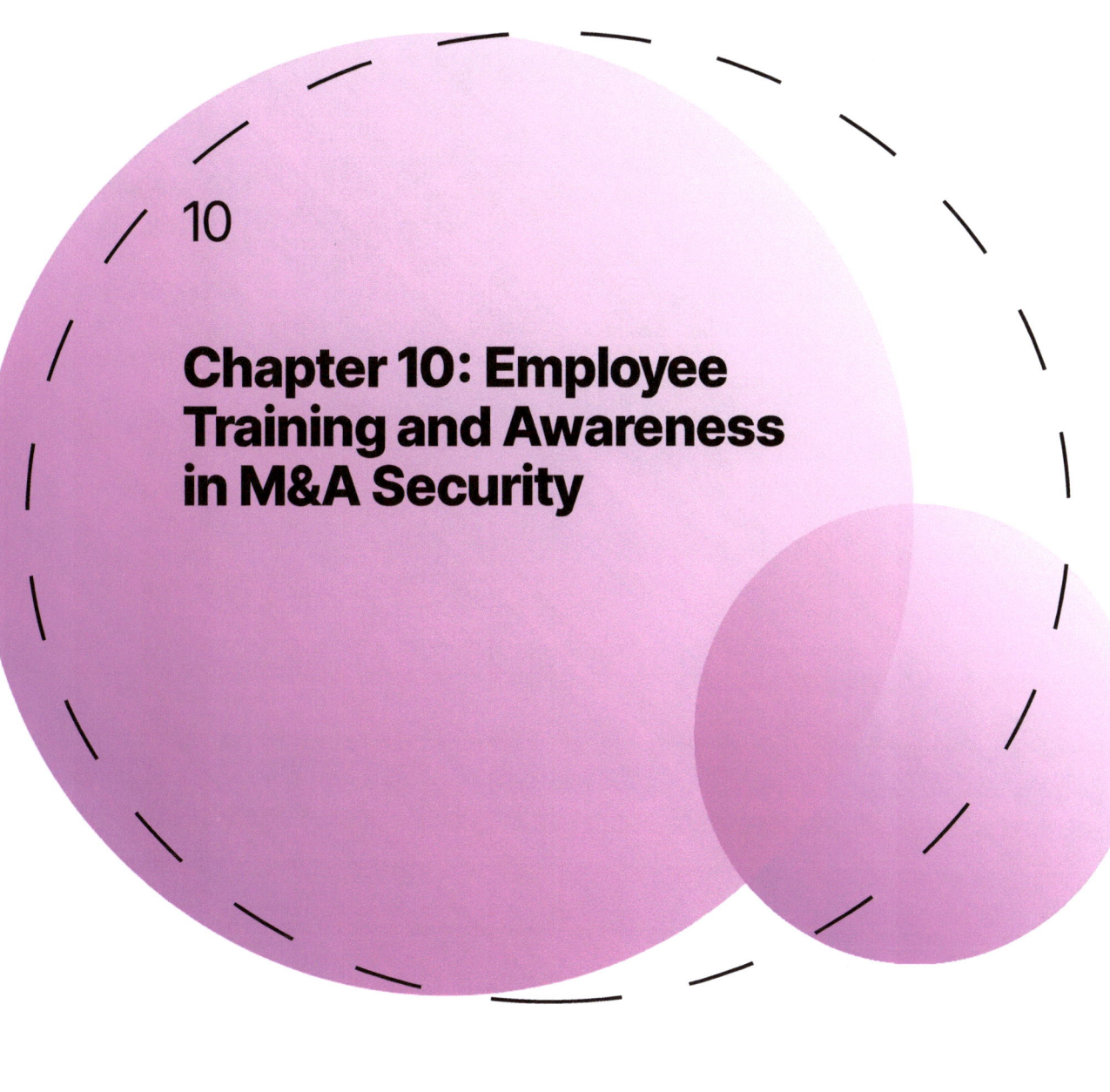

Chapter 10: Employee Training and Awareness in M&A Security

Securing the Deal: Navigating Mergers & Acquisitions Security

Importance of Security Training for Employees

In the fast-paced world of mergers and acquisitions, security training for employees is more important than ever. As companies come together, there is a significant increase in security risks that can threaten the success of the deal. To mitigate these risks, it is crucial for organizations to invest in comprehensive security training programs for their employees.

One of the key reasons why security training is essential for employees during mergers and acquisitions is to ensure that everyone is aware of the potential risks and how to prevent them. Employees are often the first line of defense against security breaches, and without proper training, they may unknowingly put the company at risk. By providing employees with the knowledge and skills they need to identify and respond to security threats, organizations can significantly reduce the likelihood of a breach occurring.

Additionally, security training can help to foster a culture of security within the organization. When employees understand the importance of security and are equipped with the tools to protect themselves and the company, they are more likely to take proactive measures to safeguard sensitive information. This not only benefits the organization during the merger or acquisition process but also helps to establish a strong security posture for the future.

Furthermore, security training can help organizations comply with regulatory requirements related to data privacy and protection. In the ever-evolving landscape of cybersecurity regulations, it is essential for employees to stay up-to-date on the latest requirements and best practices. By providing regular training sessions, organizations can ensure that their employees are aware of their responsibilities and are equipped to comply with relevant laws and regulations.

Securing the Deal: Navigating Mergers & Acquisitions Security

Overall, security training for employees is a critical component of a successful merger or acquisition. By investing in comprehensive training programs, organizations can empower their employees to protect themselves and the company from security threats, foster a culture of security, comply with regulatory requirements, and ultimately, secure the deal.

Creating a Security Awareness Program

Creating a Security Awareness Program is essential for organizations navigating the complex landscape of Mergers and Acquisitions. This program should be tailored to address the specific security risks and challenges that may arise during the M&A process. By educating employees, vendors, and third parties on security best practices and potential threats, organizations can mitigate risks and ensure a smooth transition post-merger.

When developing a Security Awareness Program, it is important to consider the unique cybersecurity considerations in M&A. This includes identifying potential vulnerabilities in existing systems, understanding the security posture of the target company, and implementing measures to protect sensitive data during the integration process. By incorporating these considerations into the awareness program, organizations can proactively address security risks and prevent potential breaches.

Compliance and regulatory challenges are also a critical aspect of M&A security. Organizations must ensure that their Security Awareness Program aligns with relevant laws and regulations to avoid legal implications and penalties. By educating employees on compliance requirements and best practices, organizations can maintain a secure and compliant environment throughout the M&A process.

Data privacy considerations should be a key focus of any Security Awareness Program in M&A. Employees should be trained on the importance of protecting sensitive data, understanding data privacy regulations, and reporting any potential breaches or violations. By promoting a culture of data privacy awareness, organizations can safeguard valuable information and maintain the trust of stakeholders.

Overall, a comprehensive Security Awareness Program is essential for navigating the security maze of Mergers and Acquisitions. By addressing cybersecurity considerations, compliance challenges, data privacy concerns, and employee training, organizations can effectively manage security risks and protect their assets during the M&A process. By investing in security awareness and education, organizations can enhance their risk management strategies, ensure cultural alignment post-merger, and mitigate potential security breaches.

Employee Responsibilities in M&A Security

Employee Responsibilities in M&A Security

When it comes to mergers and acquisitions (M&A), the role of employees in ensuring security cannot be overstated. Employees play a crucial role in safeguarding sensitive information and protecting company assets during the M&A process. It is essential for employees to understand their responsibilities and actively participate in maintaining security protocols to mitigate risks and ensure a successful transition.

Securing the Deal: Navigating Mergers & Acquisitions Security

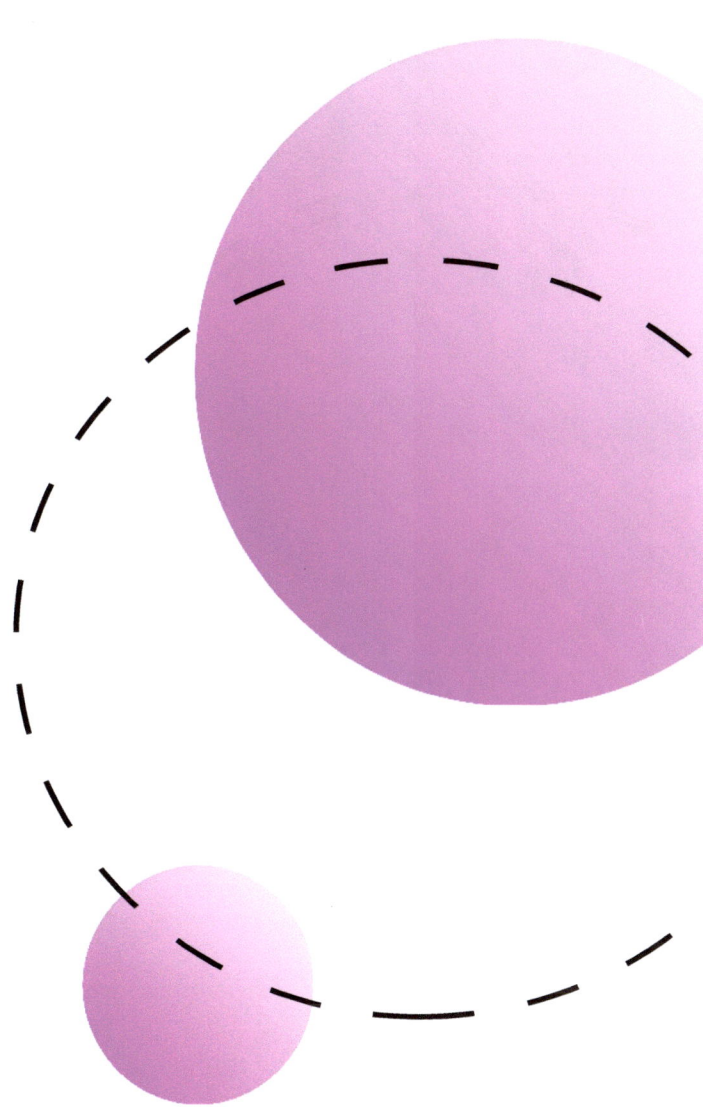

One of the primary responsibilities of employees during M&A security is to adhere to company policies and procedures. This includes following best practices for data protection, confidentiality, and access control. Employees must understand the importance of keeping information secure and confidential, especially during the due diligence process when sensitive data is being shared with potential buyers or partners.

In addition to following established security protocols, employees must also be vigilant and report any suspicious activity or security breaches. It is crucial for employees to be aware of common cybersecurity threats and know how to identify and respond to potential risks. By remaining vigilant and reporting any security incidents promptly, employees can help prevent data breaches and protect the company's assets.

Furthermore, employees should receive proper training and awareness programs on M&A security. Training programs should cover topics such as data protection, compliance regulations, and best practices for handling sensitive information. By equipping employees with the knowledge and skills needed to navigate M&A security challenges, companies can reduce the likelihood of security incidents and ensure a smooth transition during the M&A process.

Securing the Deal: Navigating Mergers & Acquisitions Security

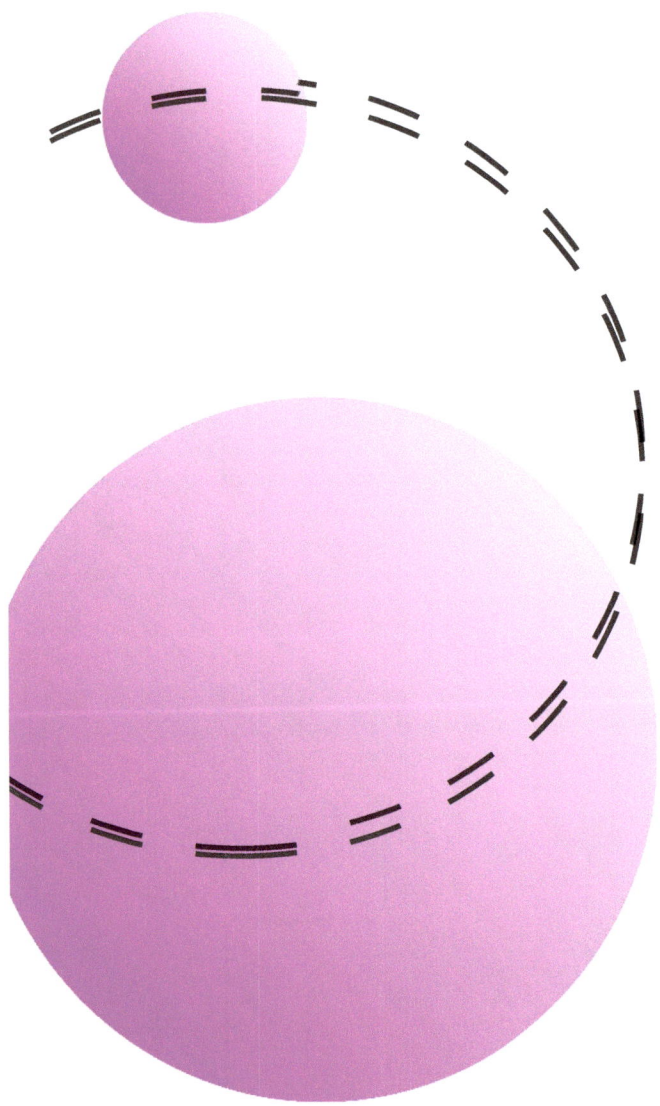

Ultimately, employees play a vital role in the success of M&A security. By understanding their responsibilities, adhering to company policies, remaining vigilant, and receiving proper training, employees can help protect company assets, mitigate risks, and ensure a secure transition during mergers and acquisitions. It is essential for companies to prioritize employee involvement in security measures to safeguard sensitive information and maintain a strong security posture throughout the M&A process.

Chapter 11: Legal Implications of Security Breaches in M&A

Legal Framework for Security Breaches in M&A

In navigating the complex world of mergers and acquisitions (M&A), understanding the legal framework surrounding security breaches is crucial. When two companies come together, the risk of security breaches and data leaks increases significantly. It is essential for individuals involved in M&A deals to be aware of the legal implications that come with such breaches.

One of the primary legal considerations when it comes to security breaches in M&A is compliance with data protection laws. Companies must ensure that they are following all relevant regulations, such as the General Data Protection Regulation (GDPR) in Europe or the California Consumer Privacy Act (CCPA) in the United States. Failure to comply with these laws can result in severe penalties and damage to the company's reputation.

In addition to compliance with data protection laws, companies involved in M&A deals must also consider the legal implications of security breaches on their contractual agreements. If a breach occurs, it could lead to breaches of representations and warranties, as well as indemnification provisions. Understanding how these legal clauses apply in the event of a security breach is essential for protecting the interests of all parties involved in the deal.

Furthermore, companies must consider the potential legal consequences of a security breach on their intellectual property and trade secrets. If sensitive information is leaked during the M&A process, it could have a significant impact on the company's competitive advantage and future success. Legal protections must be in place to safeguard this valuable intellectual property from falling into the wrong hands.

Overall, understanding the legal framework for security breaches in M&A is essential for mitigating risks and protecting the interests of all parties involved in the deal. By being aware of compliance requirements, contractual implications, and intellectual property protections, companies can navigate the complex world of M&A with confidence and ensure a successful outcome for all involved.

Liability in M&A Security Breaches

In the fast-paced world of mergers and acquisitions (M&A), security breaches can have significant legal implications for all parties involved. When confidential information is compromised during an M&A deal, the liability can fall on both the buyer and the seller. It is crucial for those navigating the security maze of M&A to understand the potential risks and liabilities associated with security breaches.

One key consideration in M&A security breaches is the issue of compliance and regulatory challenges. In today's increasingly regulated business environment, companies engaging in M&A must ensure that they are in compliance with all relevant laws and regulations. Failure to do so can result in severe legal consequences, including fines and penalties.

Data privacy is another important aspect to consider in M&A security breaches. With the growing threat of cyber attacks and data breaches, companies must take extra precautions to protect sensitive information during the M&A process. Failure to do so can not only result in financial losses but also damage to the company's reputation.

Due diligence best practices are essential in mitigating the risk of security breaches in M&A deals. Conducting thorough due diligence can help uncover any potential security vulnerabilities and ensure that appropriate security measures are in place. It is crucial for both buyers and sellers to prioritize security in the due diligence process to avoid costly legal issues down the line.

In the event of a security breach post-merger, it is essential for companies to have a solid risk management strategy in place. This includes promptly addressing the breach, notifying all relevant parties, and taking steps to prevent future incidents. Failure to effectively manage security breaches can result in legal action, financial losses, and damage to the company's reputation. By understanding the legal implications of security breaches in M&A and implementing best practices for security, companies can navigate the complex world of M&A with confidence and protect themselves from potential liabilities.

Legal Remedies for Security Breaches in M&A Transactions

In the fast-paced world of mergers and acquisitions (M&A), security breaches can pose a significant threat to the success of a deal. When sensitive information is compromised, it can result in financial losses, damaged reputations, and even legal repercussions. As such, it is crucial for companies engaging in M&A transactions to be aware of the legal remedies available to them in the event of a security breach.

Securing the Deal: Navigating Mergers & Acquisitions Security

One of the primary legal remedies for security breaches in M&A transactions is the ability to seek damages through litigation. If a breach occurs as a result of negligence or misconduct on the part of the other party, the affected company may be able to pursue a lawsuit to recover financial losses and hold the responsible party accountable. This can help to deter future breaches and ensure that all parties involved take the necessary precautions to protect sensitive information.

Another legal remedy for security breaches in M&A transactions is the option to seek injunctive relief. In cases where a breach has occurred or is imminent, a company may be able to obtain a court order to stop the other party from further disclosing or using the compromised information. This can be particularly useful in preventing irreparable harm and preserving the integrity of the deal.

Additionally, companies involved in M&A transactions may have the option to seek arbitration or mediation as a means of resolving security breach disputes. These alternative dispute resolution methods can help to expedite the resolution process and avoid the time and expense associated with traditional litigation. By working with a neutral third party, companies can often reach a mutually beneficial agreement that addresses the security breach and allows the deal to proceed as planned.

It is important for companies to carefully review their M&A agreements and contracts to ensure that they include provisions addressing security breaches and outlining the legal remedies available in the event of a breach. By proactively addressing these issues in the negotiation stage, companies can better protect themselves and mitigate the risks associated with security breaches. In doing so, they can help to safeguard their sensitive information and increase the likelihood of a successful M&A transaction.

Securing the Deal: Navigating Mergers & Acquisitions Security

In conclusion, understanding the legal remedies for security breaches in M&A transactions is essential for companies looking to navigate the complexities of the M&A landscape. By being proactive, taking precautions, and knowing their rights, companies can better protect themselves and their sensitive information from potential breaches. By leveraging the available legal remedies, companies can help to ensure the success of their M&A transactions and safeguard their interests in an increasingly interconnected and vulnerable world.

Securing the Deal: Navigating Mergers & Acquisitions Security

www.ingramcontent.com/pod-product-compliance
Lightning Source LLC
Chambersburg PA
CBHW051916210526
45473CB00006B/2037